An ABeCedarium

An ABeCedarium for Poets and Readers

Poems by
COBURN BRITTON

Alphabet by
WILLYUM ROWE

TENTH AVENUE EDITIONS
in association with
WRITERS AND READERS PUBLISHING
INC.

TENTH AVENUE EDITIONS, INC.
625 Broadway, New York, NY 10012

Managing Editor: Clive Giboire
Executive Editor: John Anderson
Assistant Editor: Peter Wagner
Assistant Art Director: Mark Muday

Copyright © 1989 by Coburn Britton

All rights reserved. No part of this book may be reproduced or transmitted in any form by any means, electronic or mechanical, including photocopying, recording or by any information storage and retrieval system without permission in writing from the Publisher.

**Library of Congress
Cataloging-in-Publication Data**

Britton, Coburn.
  An ABeCedarium for Poets and Readers /
by Coburn Britton; alphabet by Willyum Rowe.

    p.   cm.
  ISBN 0-86316-001-8
  I. Rowe, William, 1946- . II. Title.
PS3552.R498A64   1989
811'.54--dc20   89-39979
                                                     CIP

Manufactured in the United States of America

for Joseph A. Focarino

Also by Coburn Britton
Cap with Bells
Second Seasons
Lesser Goods and other poems

CONTENTS

    Prefaces
A   *Afflatus, Air*
B   *Bathos, Blank verse*
C   *Carpe diem, Clerihew*
D   *Dirge, Doggerel*
E   *Epigram, Epithalamium*
F   *Fancy, Fatras, Free verse*
G   *Gnomic, Goudy*
H   *Haiku, Heroic couplets, Hymns, Hypallage*
I   *Idyll*
J   *Je ne sais quoi, Jingle, Joy*
K   *Katharsis*
L   *Limericks, Lines*
M   *Madrigal, Meter, Myth*
N   *Nature, Nonsense, Nursery*
O   *Ottava rima, Oxymoron*
P   *Pantoum, Purple patch*
Q   *Quatrain, Query, Quintet*
R   *Rhapsody, Rhyme, Riddle*
S   *Skeltonic, Song, Spell, Spoonerism*
T   *Tanka, Terza rima, Trochees*
U   *Ubi sunt, Ululation*
V   *Verset, Villanelle*
W   *Wedge verse, Wit*
X   *X*
Y   *Yodel, You*
Z   *Z*

PREFACES

Abecedarium, alphabet book,
A primer, a glimmer, in this case, a look
At versification, poetics—what else?
(No good rhyme for "else," so I'll off-rhyme "myself.")
Britton, it is, with a Coburn to boot—
But come on, Gentle Reader, it's *you* I salute.

Abecedarian, one can be two:
Pupil and pedant, from A to Z.
Alpha/Omega, between the two,
It's all quite elementary.

Abecedarian stuff,
The guff to make one puff
From A ter Z, pluperfectly,
And huff, "Enough's enough!"

Afflatus, an highfalutin word for inspiration,
The wind that's s'posed to set one to the works,
That bounteous blow and awful swell
On me and my own rhapsody for thee.
I take it daily now (in moderation).
But the Divine Dose does it—
The sure touch of frenzy, the fire of passion
Damped to wonder, devotion, and praise.

Air, here, as light as—
Loll on a lute and sing!
Not lipped by Lydian choirs,
Alone the line aspires,
A seraph on the wing.

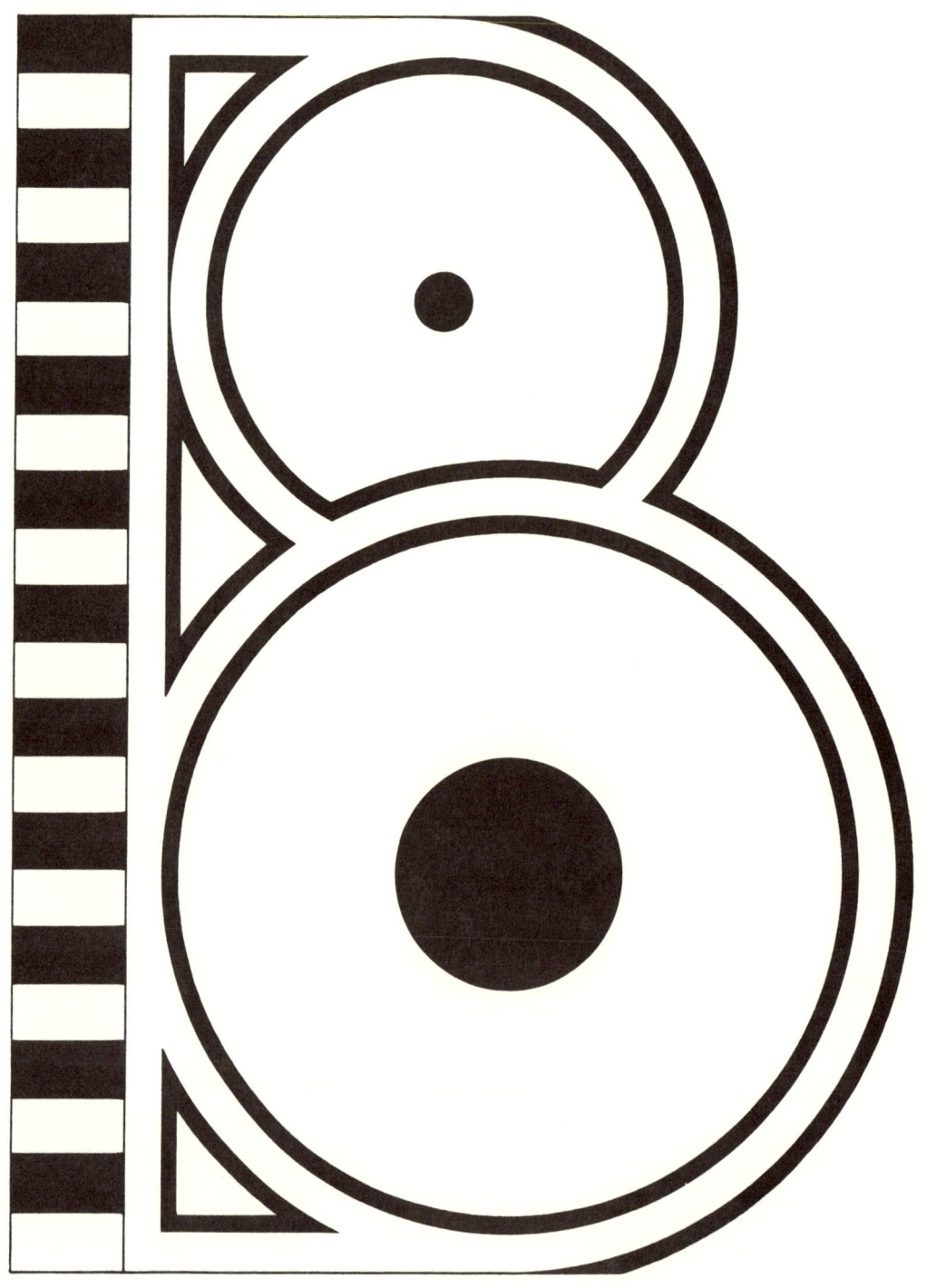

Bathos, sunk by our own English Pope,
"The sublime to the meticulous,"
I'll bring it up again, and again.
No sissy fuss, I'll scale the heights
Profoundly moved by, yes, abandoned dogs,
Lost children, lovers, sunsets, heaven and hell,
And anything else you've got to say?

Blank verse our English speaking tongues can lick
Iambic meter and five feet to shoe,
Eschewing hidebound rhyme to lace lines up.
Its stresses fit our footings, fine or loose;
Its clauses give us pauses and a form—
For saying what? My head's become a blank!

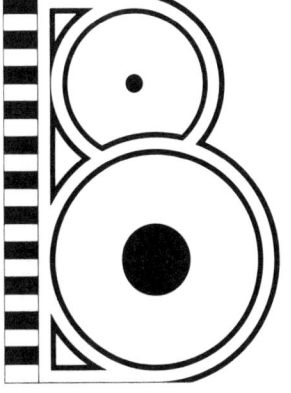

Carpe diem, seize the day,
And why not night as well?
Mow lawn while the moon shines—
Dark's dewdrops spark the grass.
But risen sun burns both away,
And we will die to tell
The vale of tears and clinging vines
That morning's glories pass.

Clerihew Bentley
Quite absently
Cross-minded his ease,
Clue-dotted his teas.

Dirge, sing for the dead lamentations;
      consoling is not for our giving.
Ring all the bell tolls;
      beat drums that are muffled things,
      not for the living.
Damn these dactyls!

Name the plague in this sod: Life,
      cured, preserved by Death.

O thou stricken Stricklands!
Paul, Blount, Charlie, Charlotte, Jackie.
Fair Oaks, d. August 11-16, 1900.

Doggerel, a female dog
Uncouth sorts hail a bitch.
They coarsely call my pig a hog,
My bog garden a ditch.

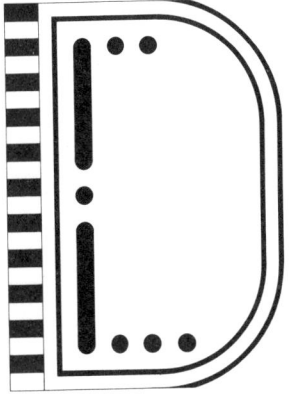

Epigram, a flash of wit.
It can be brash or delicate—
A lash, a gash, a hit, a twit.
This writ has made a hash of it.

Epithalamium, here comes the bride
Into her chamber, the groom by her side.
Outside their bed's room we will abide
Singing of wedding nights, all that's implied—
Sanction and bond's blessing, sex sanctified
By Judaeo-Hellenic boys bona fide,
By Renaissance bards, the most qualified
To keep love awake and not lullabied?

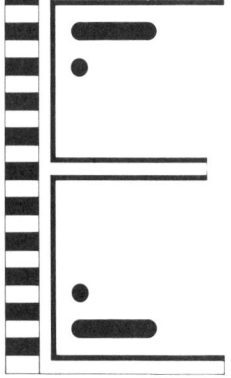

Fancy that, imagination's sibling—
Coleridge, Wordsworth, Ruskin, Croce quibbling.
It's all quite plain to me,
In fact, Reality.

Fatras: simple as the wide dome of please,
don't stop the gazer, stroke amazingly
the gleam of glee, the budding cow slips care
fully formed from bedtime stories' fables.
Augean horses round the table are
thurifying nonsense with their spirits'
aqua vitae, juiced and nectared godly,
oddly high-jinxed, sphinxes play their fiddles.
Cattle, sheep, goats rain over stars tonight
their milky sumps some heav'nly tears of joy.
Don't stop the gazer, stroke amazingly.

Free verse/vers libre—at what cost?
Say, a pound of Ezra's flesh? And
Free from what? No limits? No warp?
Dear Walt's "Song of Myself" is full
Of fallen man. Ah, but the measure is
(And this is why verse is free):
It moves us and itself as poetry
On variable feet, from slog to wing.

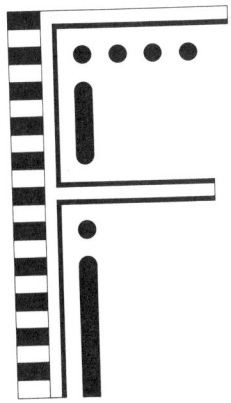

Gnomic, to speak proverbially,
Leaves me the proverbial fool.
"Why must women weep, and men remember?"
(Thank Tacitus for that germanic gnome.)
I can find a pin in a haystack.
Two of them, haystacks, there are.
Caught in the middle, I am.
Bray, ask me no questions . . .

Goudy, laud and honor,
Gaudeamus, Will Rowe, too—
Your letters are elixir,
Their font all print's purview.
You goodly grace these pages,
And guide me through my paces.
From A to Z you place us
With your types' timeless faces.

Haiku, this snowflake
resting on a cherry pit
in January.

Heroic couplets make a rare found sum:
The wee Miss Warren wedded to Tom Thumb.

Hymns are odes for gods composed
To keep them feeling well disposed
Toward mortals in their mortal hide:
O Lord, let me with Thee abide?

Hypallage: exchange, my youth for a soul?
The flower smells me,
And the zebra of my socket in the back of my foot
Is well-starred.
Let us not exchange vows—
Escape from life separately,
Taking from the gods their debts,
The gods receive us?

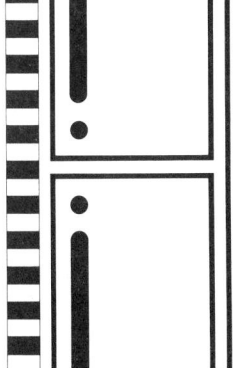

Idyll. Her room. Her scape. One room breaking
on the philtres of dawn; potion suffused;
soft crack of daylight framed, beamed
       (not too beamed), dif-
fused soft greys, pinked, fleshed light tremors
    lilting.
           Her tea cup. Her single rose
at ease.
      Her age. Her innocence. As still as
the cockroach in the corner clean as a whistle.
No Minotaur.
        Far below, the subway's rumble atones.

    O glad nooning now.
Nimbused, her ceiling is perfection.
Cerulean, the merry meridian,
azured, clear as a virgin's cloak.
No testamental tinctures.
            The bread is on the table.
The cheese in its dome.
Her diary is open to the day
     ("Yesterday, yesterday," say the breezes). The
other window is open:
the river, the voyage, the works,
playfellows and blessed solitude will she find.

    In the afternoon
             the vines swung swing,
the gorgeous garland, the every greens of spring,
and sumptuous summer, fecund fall, warm winter and
the cockroach on the hearth.
          Sundown.
The rose again.
A west wind puts her diary to tomorrows.
The window is (figuratively) closed.
Night. Bed. Dream.
Destination: Her room.
(Houston St. stop on the IRT.)

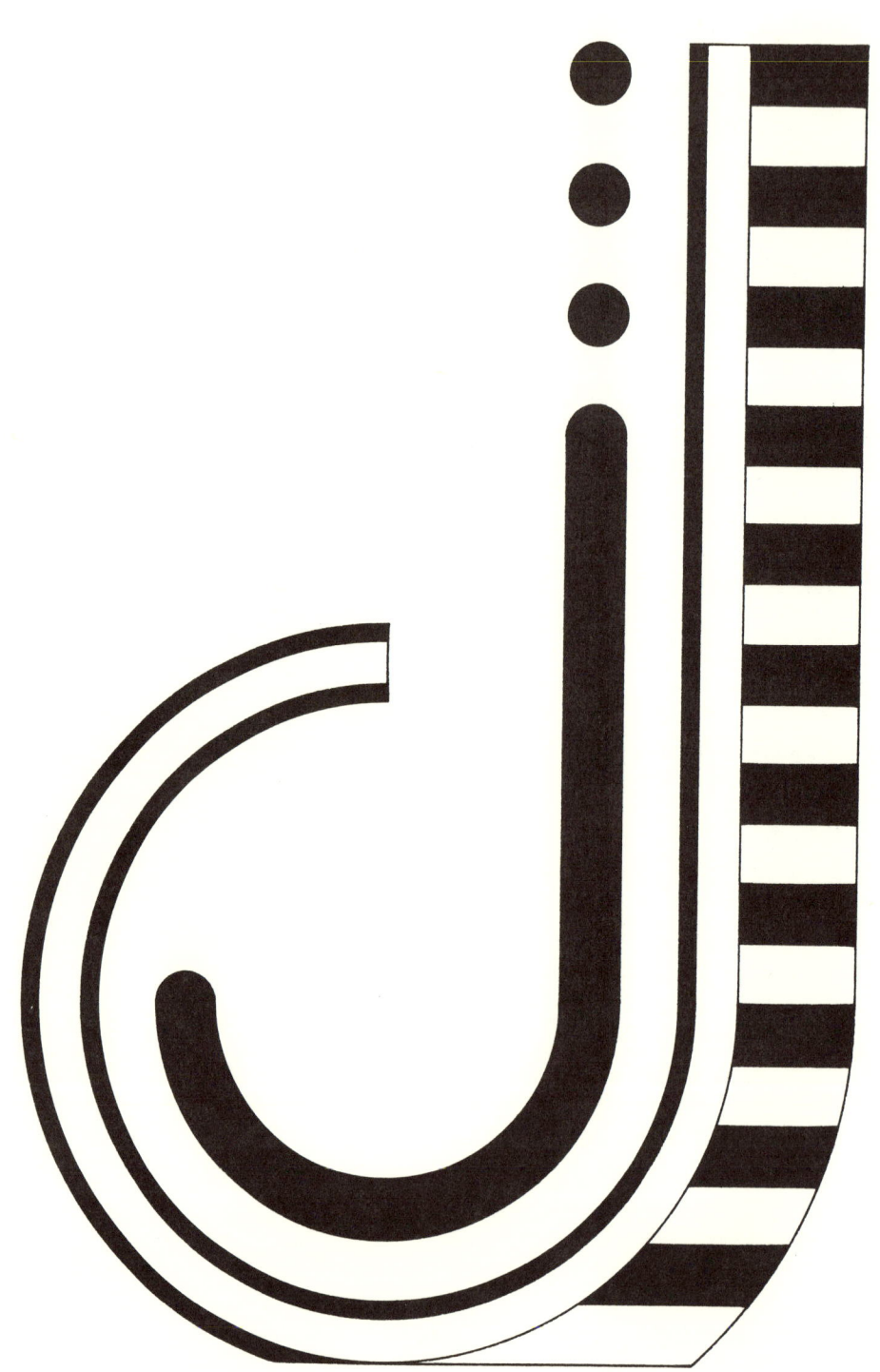

Je ne sais quoi, "I know not what a
Nameless grace possesses my face, a
Posteriori," quoth Cleopatra.

Jingle, jingle, jingle,
Kris Kringle's in the ingle,
His surcingle's a-tingle,
Ouch!

Joy to you!

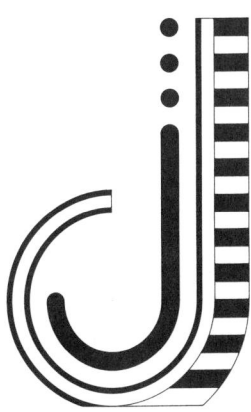

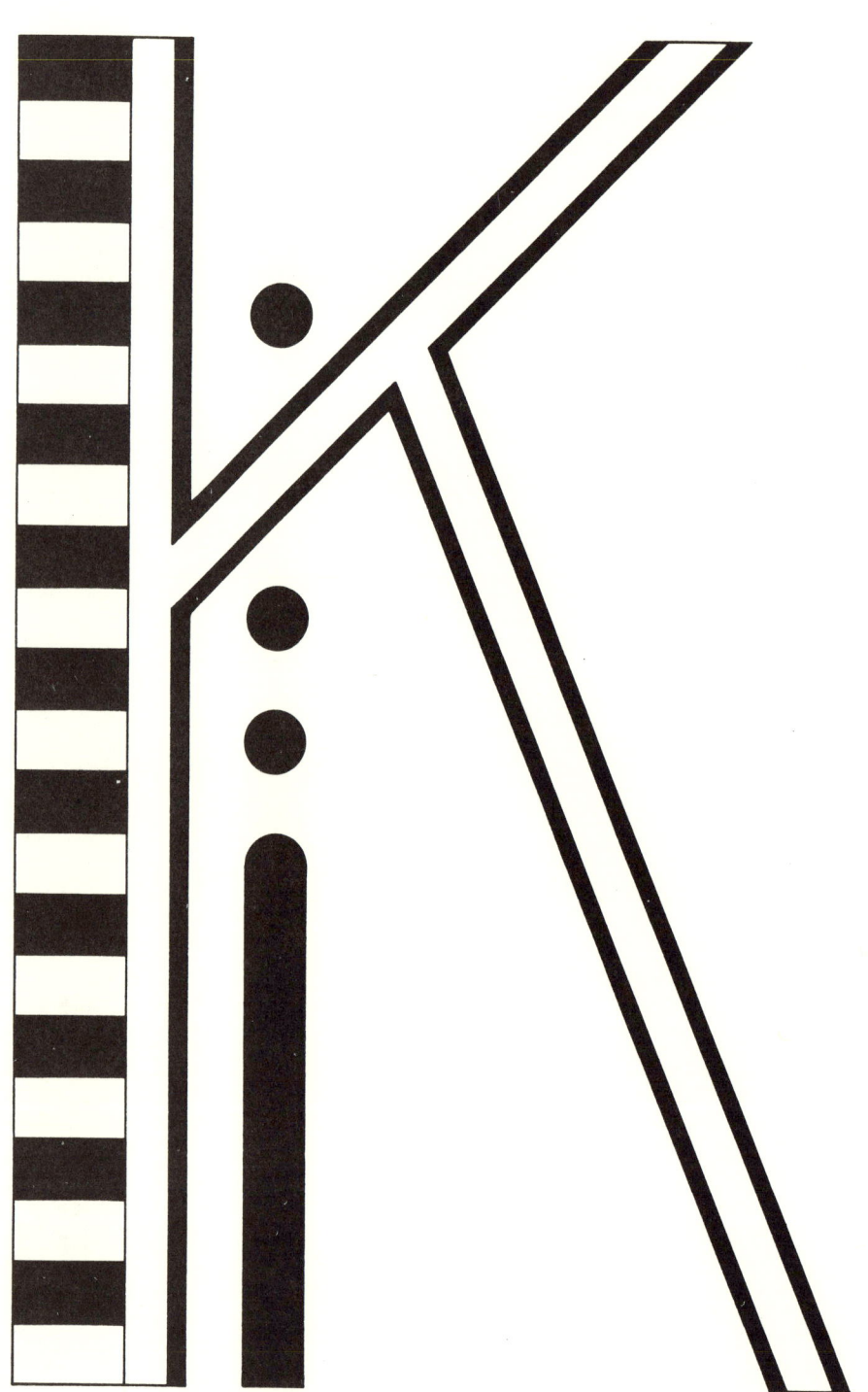

Katharsis, I avoided it at "C".
Too soon in this lineup. Too soon for me.
Now, near the middle of this -arian,
It's time for a Caesarean—
Bring it out now (no abortion, please),
Our child, our comedies and tragedies,
Small, red, wrinkled, squalling, quite appalling—
But a proper Hippocratic purge.
This babe, this nubbin, this urge to live
With tears and, after, laughter.
                                      The years
Roll by. Strengths and flaws accrue. A few
Of them form "character," so called—the do
Or die. Why what a pity! What's to fear?
You name it: lies, love, loss, noblesse oblige,
Innocence, fate, the pox, too soon, too late.
Oh reader, viewer, we participate:
We're caught, relieved, released, the expurgate.
Great friend, you're dead (the pox, this time),
      you're home.
Acquired. Immune. Deficiency. Syndrome.

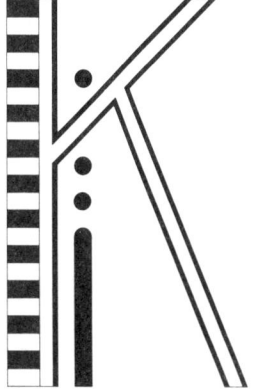

Limericks ought to be light;
But this one's about in the night.
See, it's dark. Can you read it?
Oh, come now, concede it—
Limericks ought to be light.

Lines, "units of attention" (not necessarily sense).
Lining this one out, it comes to me that there are
Lines threaded, strung, corded, roped, flaxed, clothed
Lines measuring, leveling, bounding, inheriting
Lines carrying steam, gas, water, oil, exhaust
Lines telegraphic, ionized, fished, barged, frigated
Lines distinct, demarcate, drawn, graved, furrowed
Lines ridged, seamed, penciled, chalked, penned
Lines straight, curved, real, imaginary, whimmed
Lines on the brow, soft, careworn, crow-footed
Lines of laughter, lineament, content, in absentia
Lines o' verse, a letter, punishment, rich reward
Lines of thought, conduct, policy, fire, firmament
Lines which are departments of industry or trade
Lines to destinations, of the air and otherwise
Lines of subject, assembly, glib address, confession
Lines trenched, ramparted, disposed, formed, whorled
Lines of ships, hopes, hoses, noses, roses, supposes
Lines backed, goaled, written, typed, printed, ignored.
"Don't hand me that line," said he.
"I know your line," said she.
"I'm giving you a line of goods," said I,
"All but those I can't remember. Line me!"
Lines ad infinitum_____

Madrigal sing we merrily—
May we sing this gladsome May?
Nature, love, meet carelessly,
Bringing on the natal day.
Nine months hence 'twill be offspring—
Weep in winter, weep in spring.

Meter. Beater.

Myth, someone once said I -ologize a lot,
Every experience. Why not?
Just now, a dove's lit by the window.
(There was a flood in the backyard yesterday.)
No olive bearer, it's flown to a ginkgo branch
Grown nine whistling wingflaps away, and
Ruffled 'round in the green 'round a nest.
Its mate's appeared with soft from what or where
In this city, one wonders.
      They're at it all morning, winging, ruffling
High over the pavement before the brooding,
Using the windowsill for a vantage.
Below that pair for life we'll pass, concluding
Ours. Theirs it's said's a symbol of peace
That passes understanding. Theirs, too, purity,
Gentleness, loyalty. And ours, the Holy Spirit.
A fire engine passes. Security?
The doves' whistling wings ascend, descend.
Hear it?*

* *The following week, housepainters on scaffolding*
  scared, probably, the pair away.

Nature, yours and mine. All that surround abounding,
Breathing, winking, waiting—the very stuff again,
Again, suspends, wafts, whorls, wraps of its own
The wild and tamed, the Godded and ungodly realmed,
Kingship, curiosity, elixir and effluent, deserts,
Explosion and utter calm, touching and solitude
With all and not at all. The skies, forests, seas,
Improbabilities, sudden secrets, songs and poetries.

Nonsense, cries my addled pate.
Never too early to be too late.
The screw in my head's too loose to woo—
To wit, no wit, and who are you?

Nursery verse preserves the child,
Nice and mild, or nasty and wild;
The first shall ever in syrups glide;
The worst will sink in formaldehyde.

Ottava rima's right for blending things,
Our tears and laughter mingling the emotions;
The story of one's life and ending things
In pity, fear and death, or with love's potions.
Don Juan quaffs them deep, forfending things
Until his ghostly guest stirs up commotions:
All hell breaks loose, the Don to flame is carried.
(Most everybody else on stage gets married.)

Oxymoron, foolish genius,
We call silently to thee—
Nonexistent, overween us,
Humbly let us laugh with ye.

Oxymoron. Foxy moron.

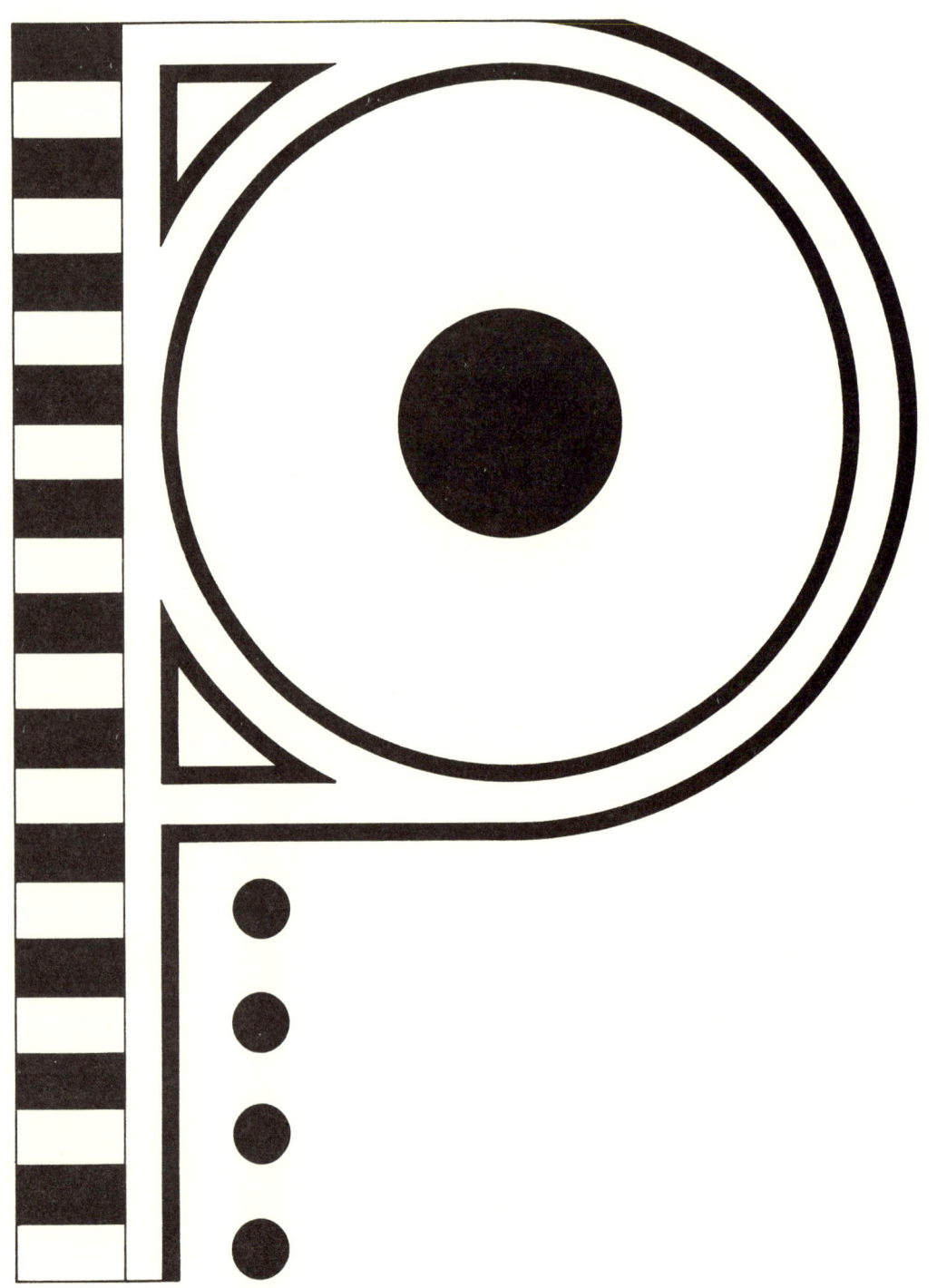

Pantoum: Begin and end me, poetry.
Give me simple songs of love and passion.
Come away, my friend, with me to wander.
There are wonders that we'll come to gently on.

Give me simple songs of love and passion.
Strong is the beating of our heated blood.
There are wonders that we'll come to gently on.
Beyond the hills and dales are star struck skies.

Strong is the beating of our heated blood.
Come away, my friend, with me to wander.
Beyond the hills and dales are star struck skies.
Pantoum: Begin and end me, poetry.

Purple patch, the throbbing red and blue of it,
The confusion of contusion 'round my eye,
Black as the berries of my mother's pie
Which, on the face of it, has made a hit.

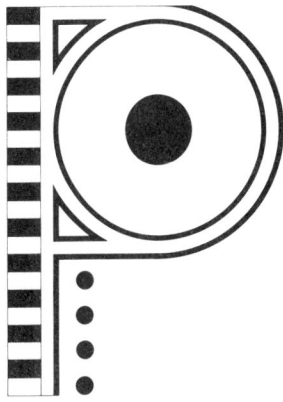

Quatrain, four lines, two rhymes, a little wit
Is helpful if it's writ to stand alone.
In this case, forty feet'll bulk a bit;
They cannot fit a simple stepping stone.

Q is for *Query*—
Whose shoe?

Quintet, a stanza, here a fiery place,
This one to warm us of the Pentecost.
Five decade days from our Lord's rise, His grace
Descended as the Ghost, a holocaust.
A perfect sacrifice, that fire. None lost.

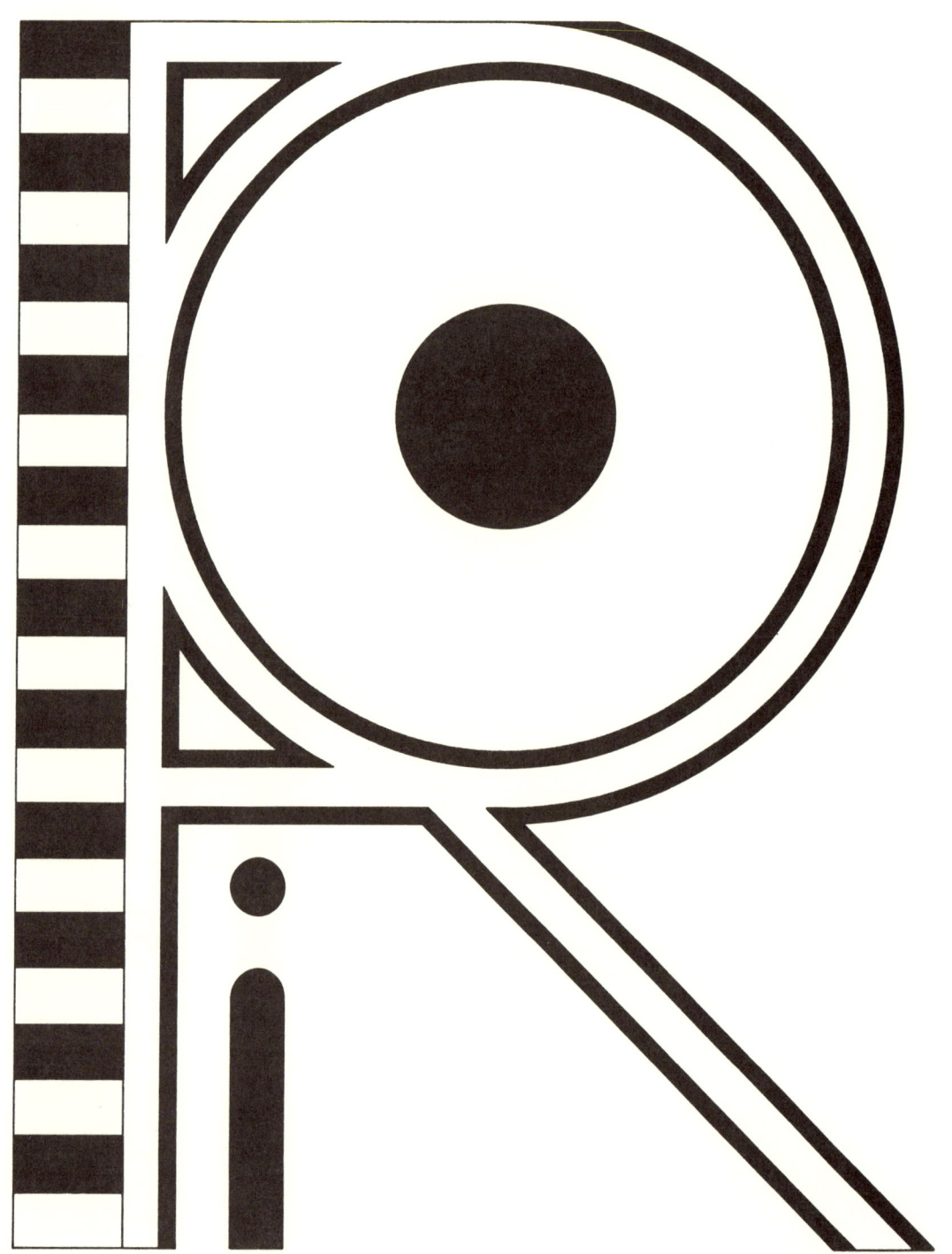

Rhapsody, off, away, velocity,
Plunge up to soaring, stoop and plummet,
Catch all sweet cacophonies,
Explosion, curling cadence, hurling
Hilarities right round the streak,
Bent, arced and in a swound
Of sweat, steamed vapor's blow
All crystal crashing, soft suffused,
Imbued, that brilliant ink pinks on
To dynamo, mosaic fracture, rapture
Tessellated, grace glimmered radiance.
Descend fire, consume us whorled,
Crossed, splayed, opened, utter, Trinity.

Rhyme. Chime.

Riddle, what is griddling,
Fries high, the middling, low—
Nero with his fiddling,
Gulliver his piddling,
O'Leary's Chicago?

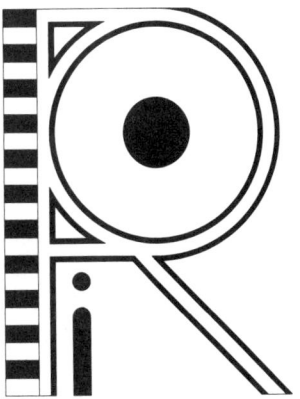

Skeltonic verse,
Reverse mnemonic,
Laconic, terse—
Nurse's tonic.
Chronic curses
Disperse demonics,
Ironic, diverse,
At worst, moronic.

Song, simple as the day is long,
Short as the shrift of a bloody liar,
Truthful as tune from a virgin throng,
One mockingbird becomes a choir.

Spell, will-o'-the-wisp, wee light, a wink.
Glimmer me meaning before the morn—
Gossamer glamour me, lightly enamour me—
Brink me, link me, before I'm forsworn.

Spoonerism: Err stir.

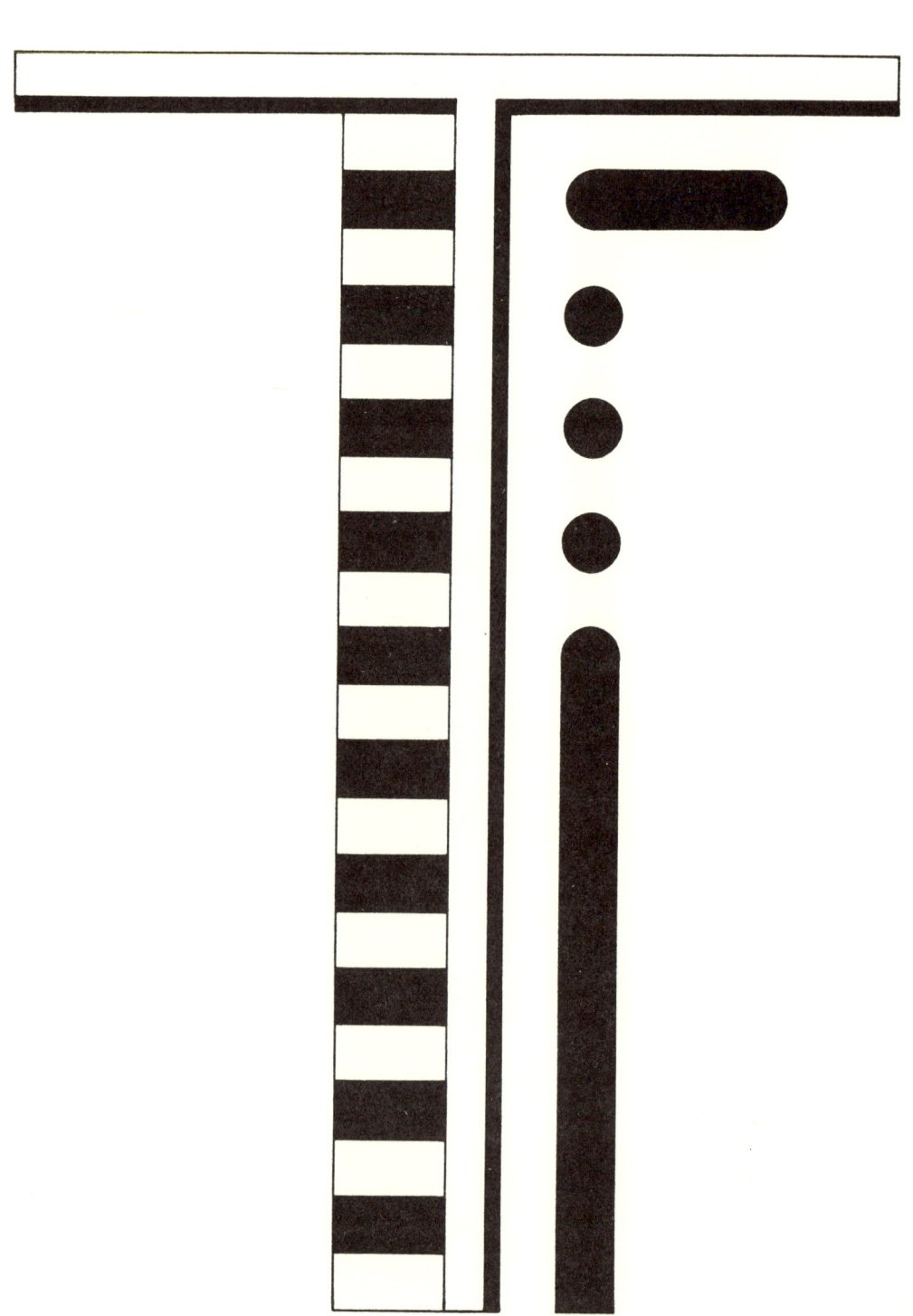

Tanka, Nippon form
Syllabic love of nature,
Lamentation too—
Star-crossed voyaging toward you.
Your due: thirty-one measures.

Terza rima, divine in Dante's book,
Boccaccio, Petrarch, to its tercets rhyme.
Our Chaucer's lady takes another look,

And Shelley's west wind with the form blows prime.
Ah, *terza rima*, English students' bane
Or glory, take your pick on overtime—

The classroom's closed; the world is yours, mundane.
Satanic mills and Arcadies befriend.
"Ah, life is passing strange," the old refrain

That *terza rima* here brings to an end.

Trochees make a dandy dancing,
When not stretched to endless prancing.
(Hiawatha had his drumbeats,
Monotonic, engine repeats.)
Here we simply take a turning,
Leap and execute some yearning—
Soar a moment, held forever—
Wheresoever, whomsoever.

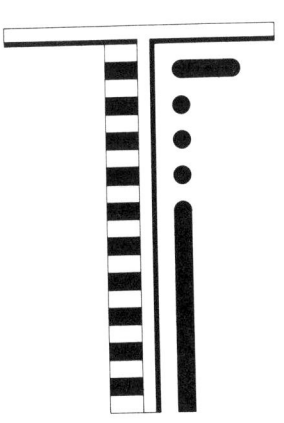

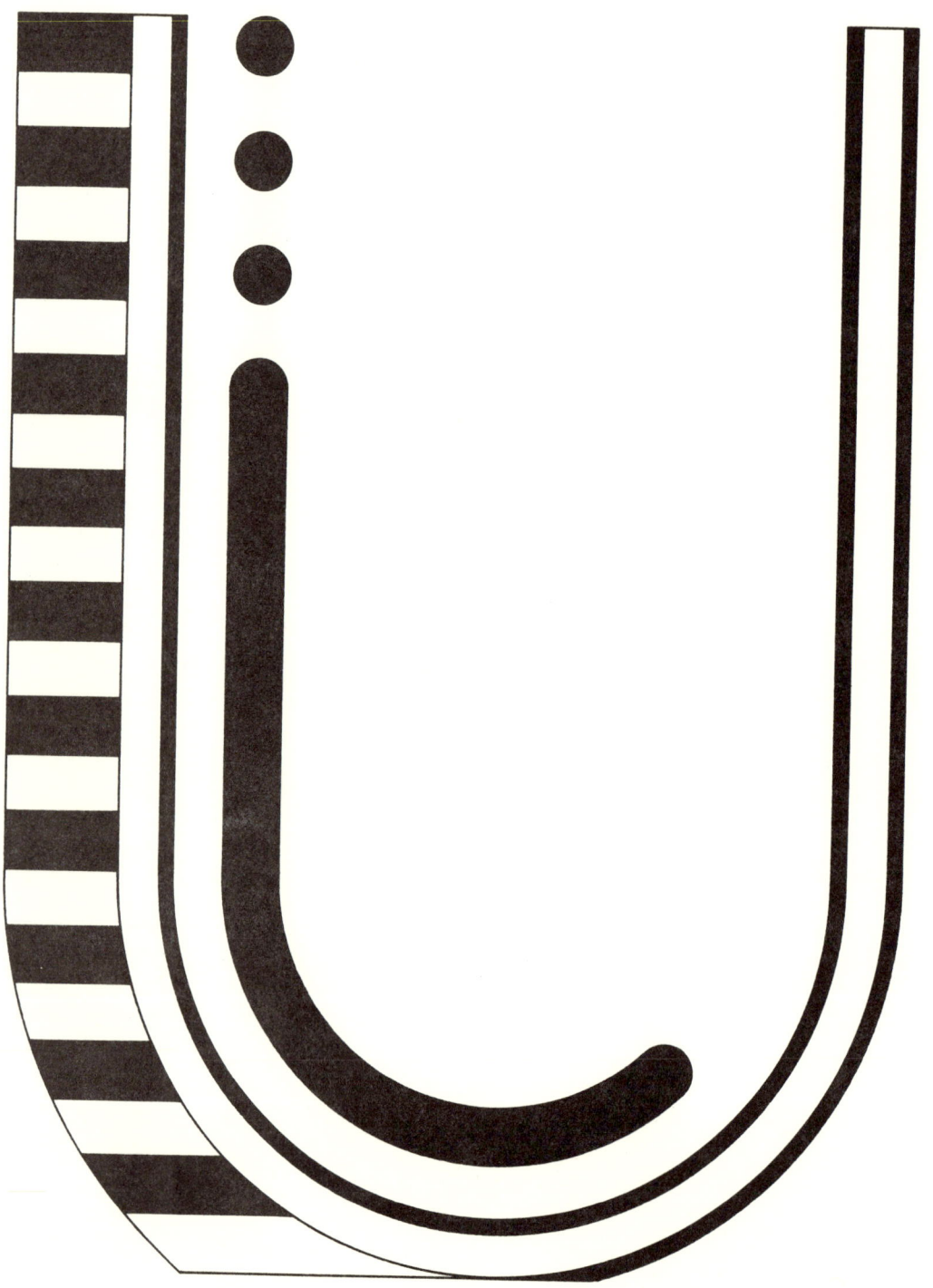

Ubi sunt, where are you?
And where am I? Are we?
What varnished glory
Passed us by?
What nacred mist shrouds better bones
Barnacled to sunken thrones?
Atlantis and pacific surges
Wash us and our demiurges.
Secondary gods were we,
Humanity in deity?
Prideful mourning! Better ages?
Better keep on turning pages.
History is what they bare,
Naked as the natal stare—
Blank as babes aborning.
Thank God for this morning!

Ululation, howling, wailing—
The harvest moon's caught
In the teeth of the coons at my corn.

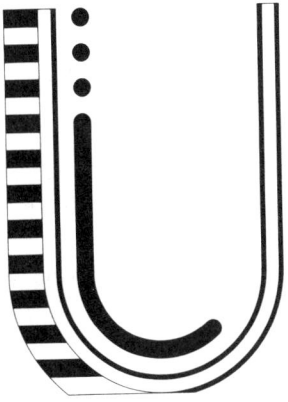

Verset. Viva vocable vendettas!
Voracious vantage, verbal vandalism,
vital vocalese, vamped vox humana,
vigilant vengeance, vibrant vagrancy,
volcanic vanity, vastly vituperate,
vinegar's vicar, violent votary,
vesseled vainglory, villainy's vested vice,
vomiting venery, vindictive virginry,
vehement vixenry, vexed varletry,
viperous vestige, verminous vulture,
vicious victualer, voiding victimizer,
vegetable visionary, viscous verbosity.
Viva vocable vendettas!

Villanelle (for Vernon C. J. Newton)

How well the willow, brash and upstart sing!
To every season your bright boughs belong.
First leaf, last laud before our wintering.

First break of color calling us to spring—
All tones follow, your sweeping falls lush long.
How well the willow, brash and upstart sing!

In sumptuous summer swagged and clamoring,
Your birded longings crown the season's song.
First leaf, last laud before our wintering.

Fecund fall's gold gauds to you imparting
The glory which your staying powers prolong.
How well the willow, brash and upstart sing!

You sound through winter's icings—a sparkling
Choired carillon, aeolian, double-strong.
First leaf, last laud before our wintering.

Belying storm-bluff blasts, the splintering,
New shoots spring up to join the windglad throng.
How well the willow, brash and upstart sing!
First leaf, last laud before our wintering.

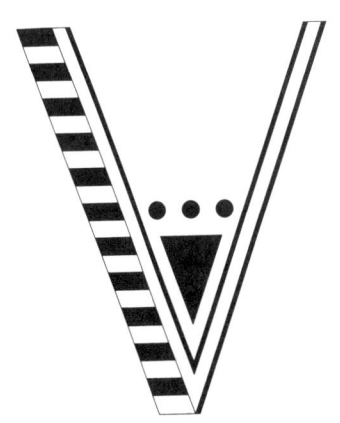

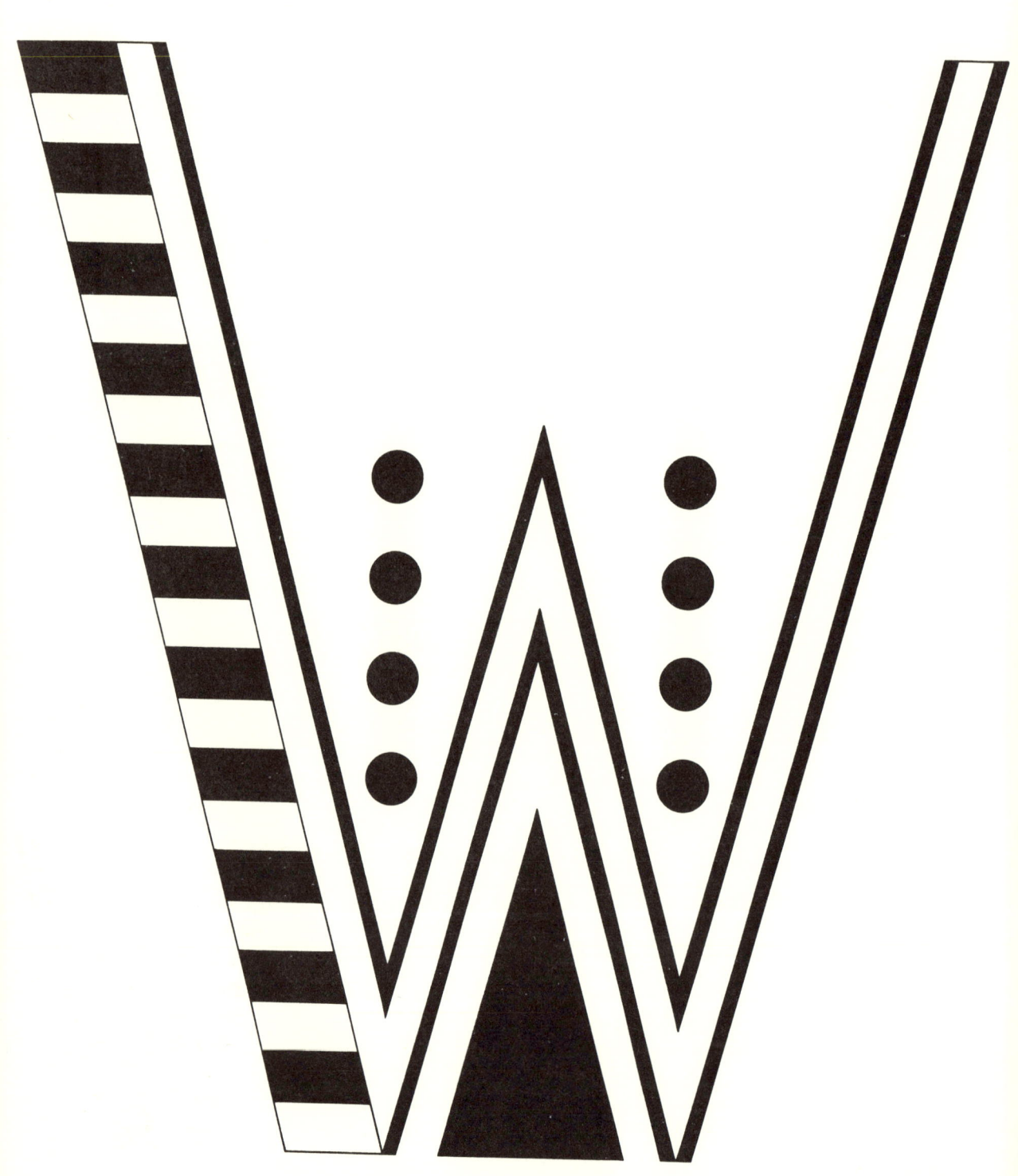

Wedge verse's a-growing alarmingly,
The fruitage entrusted disarmingly.
Sly serpent's bestowing revealingly
The apple piecrusted appealingly.
But cooking's apostate Edenically!
Now mankind degustates hygienically.

Wit, what is it?
With this writ, I'm asking for it.
Aristotle's "well-bred insolence"?
Paradox, farfetched antithesis?
Pope's "nature to advantage dressed"?
T. Eliot's "tough reasonableness"?
Levity's ally, seriousness?
Imagination, conceptual powers?
Irony's metallic flowers?
I'm asking for it, oh, I know it.
Stop me, please, before I blow it.
Don't deplore it, epitaph it:
"Here lies wholeheartedly a half-wit."

X is where we are:
X marks the spot, the letter's face, this page.
X marks the treasure chest, the rainbow's wage.
X signs Dumb Dora's name, Old Geezer's too.
X's mine, Tiresias'—to name but two.
X makes a Roman numeral, a ten.
X multiplies the few 'til they say when.
X is an unknown quantity, a thing.
X names it, presto! X becomes Something.
X, a mistake, an error, null & void.
X, obliterate, struck out, to be destroyed.
X, a cross, a shape, three rose on Calvary.
X, the Christ, the Savior; X, the votary.

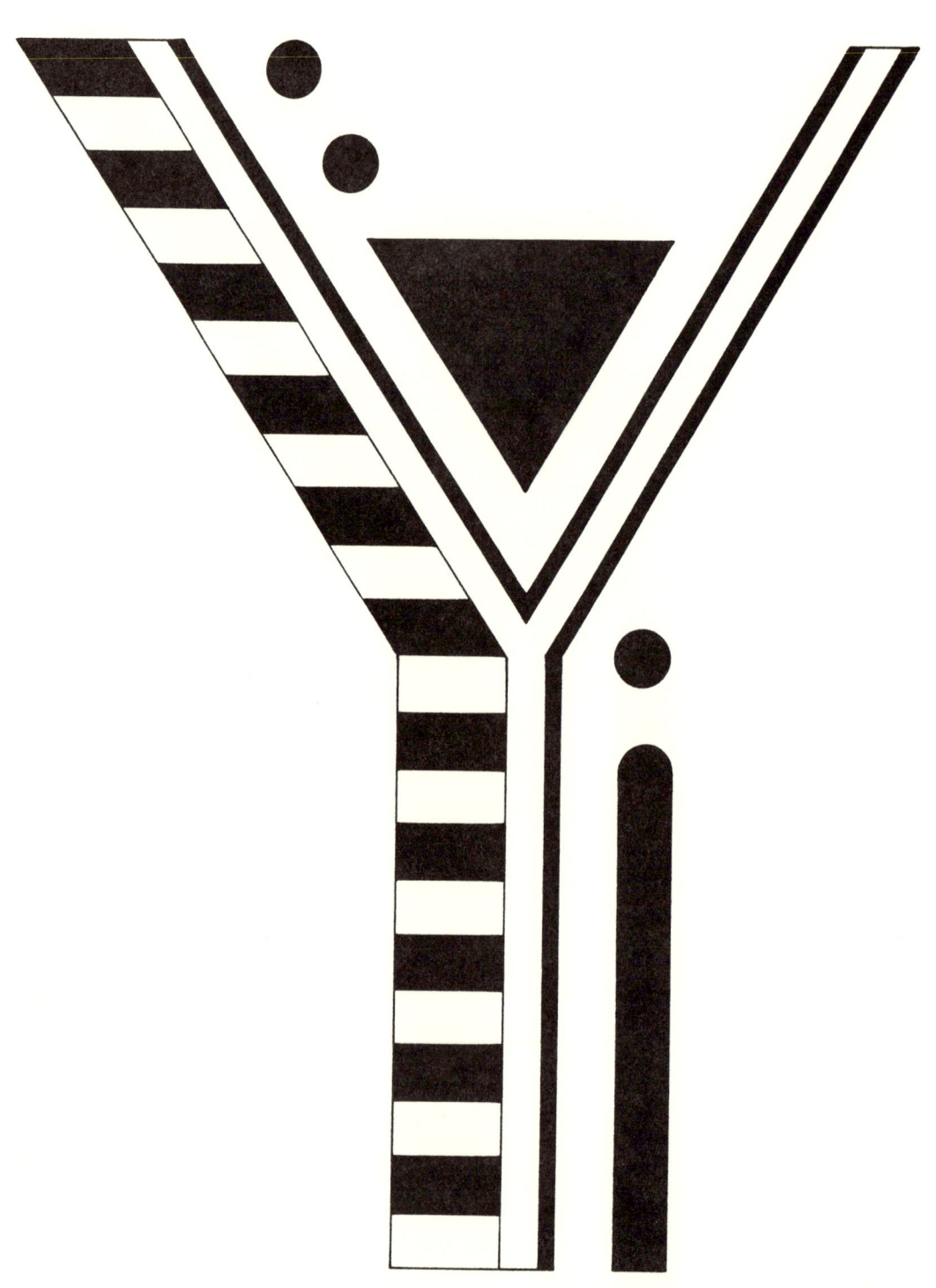

Yodel.
Tonal,
Tyrol,
Glottal
Stop!

You, Gentle Reader (rough reader, as well),
Bring life to this print, to me.
This abecedarian "show & tell"
Is my reality.
It may not be your cup of tea,
Or your meat (with a grain of salt)—
It's all I have to offer thee,
In apogee or perigee,
Nonsense and sensibility—
Poesy's treasure-vault.

Z, omega, last letter,
Alpha's nether part.
Here it's pace-setter;
Let's make another start.
The end at the beginning—
Z to A, why not, this time?
On course, full-circled winning,
And laureled with some rhyme.
That crown, your reason's noted,
Is oft a bit askew.
The head's a wee bit bloated,
The feet a load for two.
Some iambs wear wolves' clothing;
Some dactyls parry teeth;
Some puns have won your loathing—
But a true heart beats beneath
This versifier's hidebound,
Cliché riddled though it be.
(And, incidentally,
Z's also buzzing sound,
In form writ z-z-z—
Menaces and bombs abound,
Though snoozing's more likely.)
Ah, wake up! The Word's around!
To real poetry—
For each to each our love is found
From God in you and me.